KETCHUP

KETCHUP
Sopa de Gato

A WORD IS WORTH A THOUSAND PICTURES

Carlos Ornelas

Humblebee

Special thanks to Hiram Sims, Manny, Ronnie (Backstreet Poets), Kimon Haramis, Dr. Ruth Roach, Emmanuel (Sisko), Dalia Juarez, & Mr. E., for helping me believe in me.

Contents

FOREWORD
      HIRAM C. SIMS   13

PREFACE
      CARLOS ORNELAS   17

CHAPTERS

    INNER •VIEWS   **23**
      Inspiration   25
      Children of the Universe   26
      Second Wish   28
      I Am   30
      The Future   33
      Rain   34
      Bees   37
      Grateful   38
      Fly-Birds   41
      Zion   42
      Knowing   44
      Faith   46
      Tomorrow   49

    EVOLUTION   **51**
      Reciprocity   53
      Change   55
      Paint   56
      WeakDays   57
      L & S   59
      Hickies   60
      Bucket   62
      R.A.P.   64
      Corpnopoly   66
      How to raise the dead   68
      Happy Dogs Day   70
      Adios   72

DEDICACIOUS   **75**

    Tulip   77
    Roses   78
    Queen of Spades   80
    Queen of Hearts Broken   83
    Sky'Rocket   84
    Baby Angels   86
    Leticia   88
    Sister   90
    Sausage fest   92
    Circles   94
    Medusa   96
    Phantom Grace   98
    You and I   101
    Last Call   102
    To whom it may concern   104

LOVE´ATOMY   **107**

    The Girl with no heart   108
    Hmm   110
    Nice   112
    Sweet Dreams   114
    Evol   117
    Mind Fuck   118
    Pale Sunday   119
    The Mute Button   120
    She-Devil   121
    Losing Hand   122
    Negative Plus   124
    Touch   127

STRUGGLEGUM   **129**

    Us   130
    Goodlookin   134
    Underdog   136
    Knew America   138
    The Devil is Busy   140
    Things   142
    Truth   144
    Rush   145
    Whatta Day   146
    Wetback   148
    Outcast's Prayer   150
    Smile   151

DARKITECTURE   **153**
    Regicide   154
    Aggravated   156
    Pissed   158
    We the Gifted   160
    Pale Messenger   163
    Hell'en   165
    The Beginning   166
    Midnight Sunrise   168
    Storms   170
    Day of the Dog   172
    Windy Thursday   175
    T.I.M.E.   176

ABOUT THE AUTHOR   183

FOREWORD

I am often enamored with the notion of how kindred spirits meet. People who have similar talents, ambitions, and endeavors seem to be kinetically drawn to one another through a force unspoken and undefined. It is assuredly improper to discuss how I met Carlos in this foreword, but the circumstances are indeed invariably connected to the creation of this work. I was teaching a Film & Literature class for which I was grossly unqualified, but entirely interested, here at El Camino College, Compton Center. Having never taught a film class before, the 9 or 10 students who I had the pleasure of teaching were all amazing critical thinkers. Amazing in their observance of the key literary devices portrayed in those films and outstanding in their discussion of those profound elements. It was the first class I had ever taught a college that was not a requirement, so the students' interest in the subject brought me great joy. It was in that vein, the notion of what we wanted to know and learn, that I was prompted to ask this Mood Check Question one Friday morning. The film we were watching had much to do with personal ambition, as well as overcoming obstacles on the way towards a goal. I simply asked them, "What is it that you want to be?" I proceeded to answer the question first, and explained to the class that my vocational goal in life was to be a Poetry professor. A few of them laughed, as most people do, when I tell people this lofty and insurmountable goal. After hearing six of them talk about how they wanted to be nurses, and two others businessmen, when I got to Carlos, he said something I have never heard any other living soul say before that day, or since. He simply said," What you said. Poetry Professor. I want to do that too." After about 18 seconds of stunned silence, I asked him, "Do you write poetry?" He said, "Yes. I write most of it in this little book right here." That small journal, which he held with two hands, has transformed into the very book you, the reader, hold in your hands today. It has taken two years to arrive at these humble pages, but I know the work that lies herein will last longer than any of us.

The power of imagery has long been the cornerstone of American Literature. Our ability to experience the written word through various sensory details has always been the motivation which propels our desire to read. It is also, of course, the writer's ability to make us taste, touch, feel, hear and see what the characters experience that draws the true connection between the reader and the text. There is a hint of voyeurism also that lends an added level of imagination which we readers enjoy-placing ourselves somewhere in the language of the book. As powerful as imagery is, there is a new wave of authors emerging who have added the image to the text itself. This is not a new practice, as volumes of poetry have, for centuries, included random works of art within it. But a movement of authors who are creating the images to accompany their words has sprung up in this second decade of the 21st century.

These poets have assisted the imagination of the reader in forming the image which emerges from the text. This power, which we at one point, left solely to the reader, can reshape the landscape of American literature, and has the potential to change the way we experience poetry on the page.

Sopa De Gato is a shining example of this contemporary poetic endeavor. It is a beautiful and imaginative assembly of words and images that echo the creativity of Los Angeles writers. Carlos Ornelas, who has dedicated his future to Arts and Letters, has compiled his finest work into this menagerie of pain and joy. The care and precision by which he has formed, and reformed these words is an outstanding representation of what literary brilliance can emerge from Compton College. I call Carlos my "Brother in Verse" because we strive together to demonstrate to the world the honor and value of the common man's lyric.

Hiram Sims

PREFACE

I realize this is a book of poems, but I must humbly admit that I have never considered myself a Poet. Perhaps someday I can earn that prestigious title, but for now I can tell you that I am a writer in training, or a work in progress. I do however consider myself a child of the universe, meaning I am an open-minded individual, and so is my pen. But enough about that; let me tell you about this book.

Putting together this book has become a great learning experience for me; it has been a two-year, lifelong project. The reason I say that is because I began writing this book almost two years ago, but I have added a few poems that were written in my late teens, and some that I wrote just a couple of weeks ago. I have met so many interesting people, established new relationships along this journey, and discovered so many new things, which made me realize just how infinite and unpredictable this life truly is. It is an honor and a rare privilege for me to have the duty of writing about the universe based on my spiritual perception and my physical experience.

As I mentioned, this is a book of poems and songs, but it also contains pictures and art. The reason for the art and pictures is to provide a visual perspective to the poetry. The theory that words can paint pictures in our minds is one of the main inspirations in writing this book. And so I have collected art, pictures, and images that I happen to find adequate for some of my poems, and I added my own personal touch to them, as far as, color, texture and editing.

Besides pictures, the book also consists of six chapters, with each chapter having its own unique theme, but still remaining part of the main concept of the book. These six chapters in this book are like the four seasons in a year; they each have their own climate and feel. The theme of each chapter ranges from personal views and opinions of life, to the changes we all encounter as people, as well as the less serious topics of everyday living. Other themes vary from the always-popular topic of love, to a chapter that contains poetry inspired by the human struggle. There is also a chapter of poems dedicated to certain individuals, that I think some of you will find particularly interesting, to say the least. The last chapter contains the unorthodox, experimental, and perhaps the most controversial side of my work. The order in which these chapters are orchestrated is also a significant factor in the book. The arrangement of the chapters is similar to the way the colors of the rainbow are arranged; beginning with the lightest color and concluding with the darkest.

So now you know the recipe for my personal version of Ketchup. However, I regret to inform that I cannot share the secret ingredient; you, the reader, must determine that on your own. Within that final component to this poetic concoction, lies the formula to this anomalous, yet satisfying mixture.

In closing, I just want to add that this book was not just made by me, it was actually made by all of you. I just happen to be the one who wrote it. If I didn't have anything to write about, then I would have no reason to create a book in the first place. Therefore, I would like to say thank you to all of you who inspired this work, and took the time to read this introduction. I hope you read the rest of the book as well. I realize these are extremely busy times we live in, and that everything is based on technological and computerized instruments. So I appreciate all of you whom are fortunate enough to slow down for a minute and have a moment to read. Please be thankful for that fact, for there are so many people in the world who cannot afford that privilege that most of us take for granted. Thank you once again, and keep supporting the arts, for they are the only elements we possess which provide a true reflection of ourselves. Enjoy.

Carlos Ornelas
December 23 2011
Lynwood, CA

To Cielo, to the universe, and to all who inspired it.

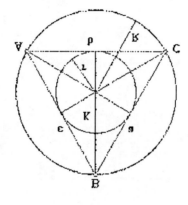

INNER·VIEWS

LOOKING FROM THE INSIDE OUT

-It's not the things we see that make us the way we are, but it's the way we are that determines the way we see the world and ourselves.

INSPIRATION

Isolation is required

For those uninspired

In order to recall,

The all, which transpired.

Only lonely may one find-

The tranquility and time,

Which is necessary

To explore a Poet's mind.

3-15-12

CHILDREN OF THE UNIVERSE

We the children,

Conceived in a musical universe

Umbilical embryos connected to stereos

Mom's stomach was my first kick drum

Songs written to the beat of her hearts tempo

Nine months later, mom is pushing and can't get me out

They had to open up her belly to take me out

Finally, I was pulled from a C-section

And they slapped me in the backside and cut my connection

Stepped into the world naked

Now I'm just another artist out here trying to make it

A child from the universe of music

Got talent and not afraid to use it

Misunderstood since the days of infancy

I guess my brain waves had their own frequency

My heartbeat varies in B.P.M.'s

And produces sound tracks for revolutions

Seeing the world metaphorically

Our dreams are made of sub-conscious poetry

As we grow from a seed to a tree

While musical rain drops fall upon me

Emotions and teardrops make oceans

I don't make love I compose it

It's a matter of picking the roses

As their petals fall down so beautiful

And they sing joyful songs at my funeral,

To the sounds of my universal musical.

second wish

There are so many things

I wish I could tell you,

But I must be careful

In trying not to fail you

So many things

I wish I could say,

Without having the fear

Of you running away

Wishing I could speak

And confess my feelings,

And write all my troubles

On the walls and the ceilings

Would you even care?

Would you even hear me?

Maybe you'll relate

Or perhaps you will fear me-

And never come near me

I wish I could tell you,

Without the disappointment

Of knowing that I failed you.

I AM

I'm an overdosed ghost-
Heavyweight shadow boxer,
I'm an alcoholic addict
My best friend and my sponsor
I'm a singer at a concert
And the number one fan,
I'm a loser and the leader
Of the number one band
I'm a reader and a writer
A lover and a fighter
A rider on a storm
The passenger and driver
A loser and an earner
A teacher and a learner,
A cold-hearted fucker
And a hot headed burner;
I am what I am.

THE FUTURE

You cannot find the future on-line or in books,
The future is there, for those who look forward.

Rain

Rain of pain
Rain of diamonds
Rain of calm
Rain of silence

Here to cleanse
Our filthy roads
Filthy streets,
Filthy souls

You make everything
So bright
Even without
The sun's light

Captivated by your essence
Mostly, humbled by your presence.
Here to wash our sins away-
Oh thank GOD for rainy days.

The Bees

One night as I strolled

Through the land of evil trees,

I was rudely interrupted

By a swarm of killer bees.

In the midst of autumn leaves

All the crows began to sing,

As a swarm of bees caress my flesh

Without a single sting,

And I died when I failed-

To find a remedy to heal me,

Without a single bee-sting

It was just the thought that killed me.

GRATEFUL

Some like to give but never receive,
Others just live with devils' deceit,

A man and his word Is a ghetto receipt,
Trust is all that He ever will need,

Those who receive and remain truly grateful,
They shall eternally sit with a plateful,

Those who receive gifts and take 'em for granted,
Only appreciate once they don't have it,

Those who will give shall also receive,
Those who deceive shall never believe,

Men with no hearts shall forever be hateful,
Happiness comes to all who are grateful.
12-27-05

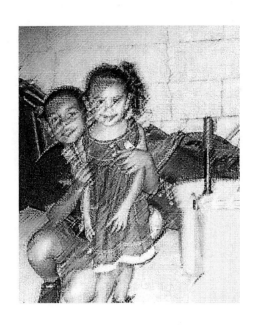

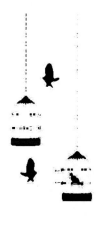
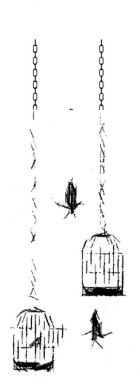

Fly-Birds

Something in me died inside

And another was reborn

They released me in July

But I never made it home

Never was reformed

Only misinformed

Years make you age

A cage makes you change.

ZION

They invite me to their house
But they never let me in
They claim equality
But I'm looking up to them.
They ask me for the love
That I never get from them
Nothing crazier
Than the irony they live.

You can have beauty
You can have appeal
But sooner than later
The truth is revealed.
You can live a lie
And get away with it
But sooner than later
You'll be enslaved in it.

They ask for my trust
And show me betrayal
While searching for heaven
They lead me to hell.

They ask me for time
They ask me for space
And here we go once again
Back to my place.

Confusion reigns
Like precipitation
Thank God for the gift
Of Anticipation.

KNOWING

It's good to know

That GOD exists

For without HIM

We are alone

Even when we are

Alone

Truly, we are

Not alone.

FAiTH

When I am able to look straight

Without fear or hate

Unable to illustrate my fate,

Faith.

Having sight

Without having vision,

Making a decision

With clarity and distinction,

I have Faith.

When no problem seems too great

And GOD is never late

Love, never hate…

That's Faith.

The power to self-elevate

Never segregate,

Instead, celebrate…

That is Faith.

To believe in what I do not see,

The powers that be…

…I have Faith in Me.

TO MO RROW

Never ask me to discuss

Why Tomorrow never was

Why the future never came

In the present we remain

Why a dream has not conceived

But somehow we still believe

So the dream remains alive

And tomorrow never died.

EVOLUTION

The Development Process

In order for a seed to grow and become a tree, it needs fertile soil, sunlight, and water of course. However, even after having all those elements that are essential for growth, the seed will remain a seed. Therefore, the most important ingredient needed for a seed to become a tree is time. Everything grows, in time.

RECIPROCITY

For all that I have taken
For all that I have gotten
The all that I've received
The nothings I've forgotten.

For everything I've stolen
And everything I've earned
For all the gifts obtained
For all the lessons learned.

For all the priceless moments
For all your thoughtful deeds
For all the world has given
Will be what it receives.

For all the things you've granted me: Respect, and love, and labor
For all your acts of righteousness; I shall return the favor.

PX
9/30/12

CHANGE

Change comes gradually
And transforms
Dark gray clouds
Into thunderous storms.

Change…comes in many forms
It is how nature performs,
That's the reason yesterday
Seizes to exist today.

Nothing shall remain the same,
Even stars will fade away,
Though you are a certain way,
That is not how you shall stay.
All you see will be replaced,
Because everything must Change.

PAINT

I'm a painter of sorts
I paint with my pen
I paint, not a saint
I am what I ain't.
Not a clee-shey,
I'm a poetic D.J.
With borders like TJ or C.J.
I'm a painter with no canvas,
No paint, no brushes
No pain, no crutches…
My pen paints what my sight touches
No smudges, no chains in my clutches
No judges,
No longer imprisoned in dungeons…
I'm just a painter of words.

*TJ refers to Tijuana, Mexico; C.J. is a street term for county jail.

WEAK DAYS

Mundee and **Toosdee**

Always amuse me

How they approach me

How they seduce me

Somehow, someway

One day they lose me

Soon to be found by

Wensdee and **Thursdee**

Groundhog Day

12 days til' Valentine's

Each one of them

Provide me an alibi

Easy to satisfy

Blunts in the alleyway

Never need diamonds

For **Frightee** and **SaddyDay**

All very similar

Also unique

These are the infamous

Days of the **weak**

I hide and they seek, they think that I'm dumb

Nah, I'm just waiting for **Sundy** to come.

L & S

Living and surviving,
Two different things.
Surviving is for peasants,
Living is for Kings...and all living things.

An inmate survives,
Shackled and confined
Seeing life through his eyes

The gratitude of living,
The habit of surviving
Two separate trains
One leaving, one arriving

A Judge is presiding,
A Doctor prescribing,
An inmate subsiding,
To living and striving.

HICKIES

Just cause I'm tipsy

This chick wants to trick me

She purposely gives me

A big, bright, red hickie

Why did I insist?

I just wanted a kiss

How did it come to this?

My girl's gonna be pissed

I've tried to remove it

With a frozen spoon

But this ain't no hickie

More like a tattoo

I even tried make-up

To make it blend in

But it didn't match with

The tone of my skin

I'm guilty as sin

I must tell her the truth

But before I could speak

I saw she had one too.

BUCKET

In my bucket,

Between death and life,

I'm in limbo

Rusted paint, no stereo,

And a broken window.

The eternal red light

On Atlantic and Imperial

I can feel the bass

From the next man's stereo.

All the women walking down the street

Ignore me

But I don't really care

I just keep on going

Broken taillights,

Oil leeks, overheating

The tags are expired

And the breaks are squeaking

My bucket may be

A big, rolling piece of junk

But your brand new car

Is still needing a jump.

R.A.P. (Rhythm And Poetry)

Rise Above plutocracy

Rhythmic Audible Phonetics

Revolution And Power

Rebel Against Politics

Royalty Amongst Poverty

Revelations And Prophecies

Respect All People

Respond, Attack, Prevail

Resplendent Autonomous Purity

Radical Abstract Principle

Reflect Artistic Potency

Report All Problems.

Rap, Hip-Hop, whatever

This is just some of the true meanings of RAP.

These are my personal definitions for it. Sadly,

The Hip-Hop of today is not R.A.P., its C.R.A.P.

Corporate Radio Audio Prostitution or you can

Also refer to them as C.R.A.P. Constantly

Releasing Airwave Pollution. You can call it hate

If you want, but I call it "Truth".

Long Live Freedom of Speech!

We, who carry the

RAP torch shall one day win.

Corpnopoly

I'm taking all property and nobody's stopping me

It's not a robbery, they call it monopoly

Corner the market airport to airport

The crooked proprietor, able to ex-tort

Roll to control, like the Anglo-Saxons

Take over corners and avoid paying taxes

My goal is to make all your assets decline

Mortgage the corporate til everything's mine

You better pay rent and make it on time

First you go bankrupt, then you resign

Then it is "I", who be the new owner

I am the one, who slowly took over

Took all the houses, took the motels

They tried to send me directly to jail

But I made bail and bought off their property

This ain't a game Homeboy, its monopoly.

HAPPY DOGS DAY

Sometimes, when you win, you lose

Sometimes, the new...

Is old news.

Sometimes,

There ain't enough booze

To heal your heart up when it's bruised

Stormy night blues,

Kisses substituted by disses

Stuck in a dream

 Where nobody listens

Nobody speaks

Their tongue just hisses*ss*

Some horrific visions I'm having-

Stormy night blues...

Sometimes, when you win, you lose

Every Dog has its Day,

Mine is today.

Happy Dog's Day. 3-3-10

HOW TO RAISE THE DEAD

First, I was paid off

Given a day off

Came back to work

Now I got laid off

And….

Everything round here

Start going downhill

Another unpaid bill

One more migraine pill

So….

Prices going up

Problems showing up

Cell phone blowing up

I'm almost throwing up

But…

I take a deep breath

And then close my eyes

Slowly exhale

Forget about time

Then…

I feel so relaxed and so in control

At peace with myself

My body and soul

Now…

I can continue

Serving my purpose

Handling business

No longer worthless

Because….

When life gives you lemons

Get you a soup bowl

Grab you a spoon

And eat some menudo

Enjoy.

ADIOS

Everyone is dying

Everybody's sick

We are growing old

And getting there quick.

We are all assistants

In our own deaths'

We the producers'

Of our last breaths'

No emotions necessary

In a man's heart

But only revealed

Through a Man's Art

Death isn't close

But it's always near

Don't get too comfy

Cause it's almost here.

DEDICACIOUS

When the poor pay homage

I couldn't afford to buy you diamonds, and could never grant your wishes. I never made your dreams come true, and never gave you glamorous gifts. I never took you out to dinner at your favorite, fancy places. I never gave you a bottle of your favorite wine, or bought you a gift card to your favorite department store. You never really got much from me, because I never had that much to give. All that I can give is thanks, for giving so much to those who give so little. I couldn't buy you any roses, and never made your dreams come true, so I wrote a book of poems dedicated just for you.

TULIP

On brown, dry leaves a tulip sleeps

Graffitied bed of metal sheets

And no attention does she seek

But yet does righteously receive

I turn her head before I leave

The sweet decapitated thing

For all that's left are tongues of red

With orange streaks is laid behead

The pointy leaves adorn her ground

As ornaments of roman crown

I turn her head to face away

On brown, dry leaves then walk away

From foolish eyes she brightly hides,

It proves me beauty never dies.

(To Sylvia Plath)

P.X

11/15/12

Humanities Bldg. El Camino

ROSES

Get your head out of the clouds

And Come back down to earth

Analyze your surroundings

And acknowledge what your worth

There is no one worthy

Of making you feel unworthy

Don't depend on them

To heal your soul when it's hurting

Don't settle for less

You deserve better than best

Never be a slave

Let them clean up their own mess

Don't ever forget

That by GOD you have been blessed

They are not deserving

Of the feelings you express

No one's good enough

To make you feel sad and depressed

They do not appreciate

The time that you invest

They don't understand

The value of your friendship

You are too amazing

For them not to pay attention

They cannot begin

To comprehend your inner beauty

They are far too simple

To be given such a duty

But no matter what they do

They shall never put you down

Because strong, beautiful roses

Always rise above the ground.

2.26.10

(To Kima, Cielo, Lulu, to my nieces, mom, and to all the roses)

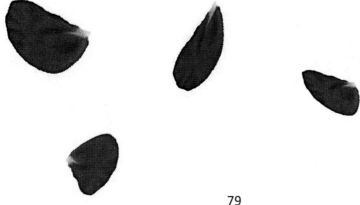

The Queen of Spades

She came to me

Like a dream.

Like four Queens

And I was the Joker,

POKER*! !...*

We make A

GŌŎ̱d PĄiR

So simple, yet so rare…

I just wanna' pull Her hair,

But it's a **f**uLL <u>H</u>OUS<u>E</u>**..**

Up in here.

So hard to touch,

I just wanna be the ACE

In Your Royal Flush…

Life is a Game of Cards,

The Ace of Spades and the Queen of Hearts.

To the queen of hearts.

The Queen of Hearts Broken

Royalty of heartache, murderess of dreams
Cardiac arrester, King of all the Queens
Witty, weeping widow; led by loyal blindness.
Tears that flood the pillow, of her royal highness;

Wolf-Hyena princess; dressed as Lioness
Keep the hearts of victims and discard the rest
Hollowed, emptied chest; no eternal rest
Victims left alive, plead for right of death

Walk around possessed, by the thought of SHE
Queen of hearts broken, Killer Majesty.
Banished from your Queen-Dom, others chose to leave
Some have tried to play with Aces up their sleeve.

None have ever beaten you in a game of hearts
Many played their fortunes, others played their parts
You just take their cards; laughing in their faces
Flashing triple Queens, at their pair of Aces.

Such a cruel perspective, such an evil wit
None but SHE can master such a detrimental gift
Pretty, vile, and swift; cunning and relentless
Someone broke her heart when she used to be a Princess

To the heart broken

Sky.Rock.Et *(To GraySky.)* 2.9.10

I got a little homie, a crazy, young kid

Who watches cartoons and plays video games.

She sings in the shower, she sings in the bed

She sings in the yard and sings in her head.

That's my little homie on a big sugar rush

She has a sweet voice but she talks too much.

"Little homie hush!" She drives me so nutty

She Gets on my nerves so I check little buddy.

You have to learn manners, little home girlie.

I give her advice like a private attorney.

I tell her about life, I tell her about the world.

I taught her to respect, And to be a super girl.

I wonder if she listens, I guess time will tell.

But she never shuts up like she eats Duracell's.

The energizer bunny don't have nothing on her.

She might talk his ears off, and give him gray fur.

That's my little homie with no money cares

I'm trying to pay bills, she wants gummy bears.

We make a funny pair, me and little homie

We watch a little "Nick" And then a little "Kobe"

At nine, it's bedtime, Good night little girlie

You have to go dream now and wake up real early.

So you can go to school, with your crazy little self

Bye, bye little homie, Go bother someone else.

Baby Angels

The day of the dead

Walking through graves

Bottle of Tequila accompanies me.

Searching for her tomb

While singing a song

Of "eternal love"

Over and over.

I place a white rose

Upon her tombstone

And quietly mourn

In the children's cemetery.

-to my baby angel, M.L.O.

Leticia

A free spirit was she

The most beauty any man's eyes could see

The star that shined upon me

The life that was missing

From earth was inside her.

My inspiration and my goal, was her

The definition of a human soul

God didn't even have a mold for her.

Everything new was old to her

I could write books about her

But they never could describe her

Accurately enough.

She was the love

Everyone wished they had

The rare butterfly

No net could ever trap.

Everybody's favorite

Immune to the hatred

A perfect masterpiece

Which the Lord himself painted

I'm just proud to be related

To a girl like her

Never met a soul

Who walked the earth like her

Her name shall forever be remembered

Between the first day of the year

And the last day of December

That's when she went away

Suddenly the sky turned gray

And there were no words

I could say to make her stay

And roses transformed into plastic,

Angels shed tears from the sky on her casket

And suddenly

Nothing made sense

It's been that way ever since

She left

Like a golden sunset

Now she only lives

In eternal memories of us

Nobody to understand us

But I miss you Lety

And I always will

Fresh, red rose

Shining on a high hill.

SISTER

Someone who is always there

Even when she is not near

Someone who is strong and fair

Never hesitates to share

One who is the first to care

So traditional, yet rare

What a privilege to me

To be close to one like she

A Lady, Woman, Mother, Friend

All the things that she has been

The light of the world shines in her eyes

And it hurts me when she cries

An example of God's love

When I feel my sister's hug

He put you here as a blessing

When this life becomes depressing

You are the one who guided me

When my young eyes could not see

You are that which proves to me

What a true woman should be

Made me strong enough to speak

When the world had made me weak

Taught me how to be a parent

Made it simple and transparent

Game me honor, gave me pride

To be standing by your side

Mended pieces of my heart

When you saw it torn apart

So much struggle through the years

But you are still standing here

The world is yours…go get it

Sister you have helped to raise me and I never will forget it.

You are the reasons'….

Why my heart has eight different pieces

Although the world may be filled

With misses' and misters',

It's hard to find any one

Quite like my Sisters. 2-19-10

Sausage fest

To my Homies,

Respect, success, and nothing but the best

That's what all of you deserve and so much more

I salute you Vatos with my right hand always

Because loyalty is higher than royalty,

Brotherhood is stronger than income

Who else could support me

When life would divorce me,

My Homies.

We got about a thousand stories

Of defeats and little glories

We may laugh, cry, or lose our selves

But we walk with Power always

Handle your shit like you always do Homies…

And don't even trip on them phony's

We can spot them miles away

But there's no challenge we can't overcome

No job we couldn't get done

Walked under moon and sun

We can shoot pool or gun

We can stress out or have fun

Fathers and sons, brothers, cousins, uncles

We can be sober kings or drunk Lords

Whether we be near or far

Do what you do and get yours homie

Cause' you know I'm getting mine

Rain or shine all the time, no question

We be the apostles

Of New Jerusalem

Only God knows'

What the future holds for us

I'm just glad to have someone I could trust

Me and my Homies clownin' the whole world

But remaining humble.

If ever the world come and get'cha

I share my last cigarette with'cha

We can share lessons, count blessings, and strive for excellence,

Nothing but Respect, Bomb Women, Big checks,

And Big Bottles of the good shit…

…To all my Homies.

CIRCLES

Sextant: *1) An instrument that measures light, stars, and the Sun's radius.*

An instrument of measure

A ruler, a scale

A clock, a calendar

Thermometer, barometer

A foot, a sense;

Instruments of measure,

A ballpoint pen

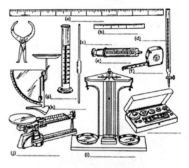

Counts the amount of pressure.

Like a simple mirror

Measures perception,

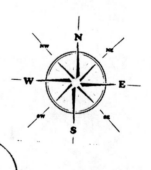

And a small compass

Can measure direction

Hearts get broken

When they measure deception

To measure the light

You must use a sextant.

It's just like seeing

The six sides in a circle

Like a star with six points

Inside of a circle.

The measure of light,

Time, and gravity...

Is done with a circle

Expanding gradually.

The eye uses vision

To measure the distance,

The clock uses digits

To measure the instants.

To measure the light

You must use a sextant

Like six Steve Urkels',

I'm speaking in circles. 2-9-10

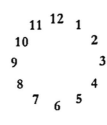

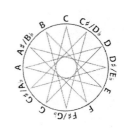

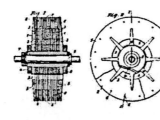

To Nikola Tesla

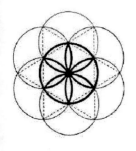

MEDUSA

Provoking me,

You are accidentally, provoking me

Or could it be the hands of fate

Gently stroking me…

The truth revealed from

Careless, outspoken me

Or could you simply be defined

As timid, yet divine

And do I dare publicly share

What secretly is mine…

When I got you on my mind.

Phantom Grace

Fallen from grace

Headed towards pale shades of gray.

Everyone is against you

They all want to judge you

Once upon a time

You were worshiped like an idol

Ever since you were a child

They watched and followed you

The world was a hummingbird

Feeding off your nectar

You gave so much

They all had a bit of you

You thrilled them all

And blew their minds off the wall

But they said you were bad

When you were invincible

They even called you dangerous

And made you invisible

And all those who praised you

Turned their backs on you

When you needed them the most.

So many accusations were lashed upon you

So much humiliation you had to endure

No wonder you went under,

So many changes.

Robbed you of your childhood,

Punished you at manhood

Betrayed by those you trusted

So misunderstood by the world were you.

They could never fully,

Comprehend your genius.

So every time you fell they laughed,

Every time you cried they cheered.

Jealous of the way you projected

The gift God gave you

A gift so great,

That it brought out the best in you

And eventually

Caused the death of you,

For it was too much to bear

And those who once judged you,

Cried tears of shame

For your death reminded them,

That in the end

Were all the same.

2-11-10

To Michael Jackson.

YOU and I

HERE WE ARE,

You and me God

Against all odds

Facing the truth,

The fakes and the frauds.

Sometimes it feels like

It's really just me…

But then You help me see,

What is reality.

Variety of sorts,

Come up's and shorts

Seems like everyday life

Is based upon courts….

Judgment,

I see goals but can't touch them,

Just another "Yet" that I have not met

Perhaps YOU are upset,

For my recent behavior,

I guess that's why I'm lost

And You are my Savior. **4-1-06**

LAST CALL

Liquor drinking man

Mumbled in his thinkin'

Swear to the lord he ain't drunk-

He's just drinkin'

Cognac cologne, Corona aroma

Whisky on the rocks, no Coca-Cola

Liquor drinkin man

Tipsy in the City

With a green olive

On his dry Martini

Red and white wine

Make his life dandy

But prefers his girls

Margarita and Brandy

Liquor drinking man

He could have been a comic

Admits he's a drinker-

Not an alcoholic

The King of gin and tonic

The champagne champion

The emperor of Scotch

The coke and rum captain

Duke of drunk driving

The D.U.I. Don

Sinatra of Vodka

Merlot Genghis Kahn

The thrilla of Tequila

Big Kahuna of Kahlua

The Whisky Jehovah

The malt-liquor Buddha

Down in Australia with a Pint of brew

Fosters in the pouch

Of a Kangaroo

If you ever see him

With a bottle in his hand,

He ain't drunk

He's the Liquor Drinking Man.

To Del inspired by Mr. Albert Collins

To whom it may concern

To Whom It May Concern, I write

To Whom It May Concern, I say

That this will be my final night

For my true love has gone away

I curse the day when we first met

I curse the day when we first kissed

I curse your lips so soft and wet

Those lips that I will always miss

Goodbye cruel world goodbye to all

Goodbye graffiti painted wall

You left me lonely, yes you did

You left me like a mom less kid

Is one thing in this world I learned

That love is fire and it will burn

Everyone dies now it's my turn

Goodbye,

To whom it may concern.

To Jonathan Flores R.I.P.

LOVE·ATOMY

The ancient practice of bloodletting

Prior to the technological advances of modern medicine, the most popular remedy for almost any illness was a technique that involved administering syringes into a vein or an artery and releasing a significant amount of blood from the system in order to relieve the heart from high blood pressure, get rid of deceases, and even evil spirits. The procedure was called Bloodletting. To some of us, Poetry works the same way.

THE GIRL WITH NO HEART

She is the girl with no heart

She is a walking fortress surrounded by a petrified forest

She and her force field move in unison

The only thing she lives for is the aroma in her never-ending coffee cup.

She has disposable acquaintances and a collection of compliments.

She has attractions with no attachments

She is a lonesome king in a kingdom of lesbian queens

She is the girl with no heart

She is smart but at times she pretends to be stupid just to see what it's like.

She is scented of a gloom perfume which contrasts her smile and her spirit

She is immune to the intoxicating fumes released by the arrows of cupid

And has vaccine shots for the love-bug

She speaks with an angel's voice

Yet she has neither mercy nor compassion for her suitors.

She picks her men like she picks her afro

Delicately, with the sensuousness of a blind couple making love;

And gradually, with the patience of an orchids lifespan.

She keeps them in her orbit, but never in her atmosphere

She pours their souls into her coffee

And tosses their bodies like empty sugar packets

Back into the populated parts from which they've sprung from.

She is just and unmoved by grooves

Her emotions have graduated from her and now study abroad

And though they sometimes come to visit

On odd and sundry instants, they never stay the distance

She thinks she loves her art,

But she only cares for the aroma in her coffee cup.

She is the girl with no heart.

4-10-2012

HHMM*!?*

Have you ever needed
Someone to the point
You think you love them?

Have you ever hated
Someone to the point
That you become them?

Have you ever worked for
Something til the point you
Couldn't get it?

Have you ever thought
Of someone til the point
You say, forget it?

NICE

Must be nice to be you
Not a care in the world
Never see what you do,
All the pain that you give-

And the people you hurt
Are the ones who protect you
But you don't have a clue
Must be nice to be you

Your material dreams
And the things you possess,
Make you blind to the fact
Happiness is priceless…

But I see you don't care,
Always doing your hair
With your phone and shampoo,
Must be nice to be you.

Sweet Dreams

In my dreams of sweetness

Kissing you is like kissing bonbons

Like eating cool whip without swallowing

And licking rainbow sherbet ice-cream on the beach

When the heat reaches 108 degrees

You are diabetes sweet,

You are the peach on the tree

That seems impossible to reach,

The one I been dying to eat

You got me messing up my speech when I try to speak…

I have dreams of your kisses,

Kissing you is a dream,

In a world where the streets are made from jelly beans

Your hair is made from spaghetti strings,

Lips made of chocolate mousse

It rains orange juice

Your nipples taste like pink starbursts'

As we bathe in strawberry quick

I taste your fingertips of licorice

Neck tastes of cheesecake, legs of candy flakes,

Thighs of red gummy bears and your bellybutton tastes

Of boysenberry jelly on IHOP pancakes

Kissing you is dreaming

Dreaming of your kisses

Dreaming I'm an inmate

In your mocha flavored prisons

The buildings in the city are made out of Jell-O

Oxygen of cannabis maintains a fellow mellow

Your tongue so sweet, I never want to let go

The trees are marshmallows, the cops look like Elmo.

But when sweet dreams end, I wake up in this hellhole

And find a white, chewed up pillow

Next to my elbow,

Oh- Hell no!

10-16-01

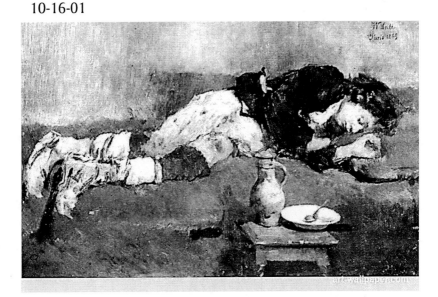

EVOL

Love is not just a word that people say
Love is what I feel for you everyday
Love is the reason why I can't forget your face
Love is the reason why we gave each other space

Love is the reason that your lips I can't touch
Love is the reason why it hurts so much
Love is the reason that I want you so bad
But Love is the reason why I wish I never had

Love is the reason why today feels lifeless
Love is the reason why it hurts me to write this
Love is the reason I'm letting you know
I Love you so much, I'm letting you go.
2.14.10

MindFuck

Honey dipped blondes,

Chocolate chip brunettes,

Mahogany redheads

And Marlboro reds/

Attractions, subtractions

And fatal attachments

Devotions, abortions

And painful contractions/

Drunken with passion

Drawn by her fashion

Kindly seduced

By the way she is glancin'/

Imagination dancin' with lust,

Unable to discuss,

Questioning whom to trust/

"Baby can I fuck?"

No, not this time…

…I just want to

Make love to your mind.

PALE SUNDAY

Pale Sunday night

Pale Sunday moon

She returns back to life

On a pale Sunday night

She came like the mist

Lonely and cold

To say that she missed

My body and soul

She spoke from the heart,

I suppose

And approached me

 Without coming close

Leaving bite marks on my skin

As if to always remind me of sin

To always remind me of when

And take me to places I've been

Then she's gone

Under dim, faded light

Of a pale Sunday moon

On a Pale Sunday night.

The Mute Button

You won't understand why I choose it-

    I'm spending Valentine's Day without Music.

Celebrating Life and everything around it

    If I never took the time, never would have found it

All we ever need to survive

    Are the simple things...

Why bother with any-

    -unnecessary promises that can't be kept.

I chose instead to resurrect,

    In order to live again

No Music on Valentine's,

Not this year

I chose silence

No more noises

Sometimes, voices can be Poisonous

    To the hearts of Men.

No Music will play

    On Valentine's Day.

2-11-10

SHE-DEVIL

Enter me said she to me

In a vulgar, jazzy speech

I proceed, intrigued to see

What about the hell she be

Sexy, scary, fearless, real

Classy, nasty girl appeal

Climax lasts eternity

And her name be Poetry. 4-6-02

LOSING HAND

Sometimes when you win… you lose

Sometimes the old is bad news

Sometimes it's best to let go

Of the one you need the most.

Better to count your losses

And know you have nothing

Than to expect a winning hand

And never know if it's ever going to come.

Sometimes, you just gotta let it be

And let nature take its course.

Find the bright side of darkness

And the kind side of convicts

When you lose it all

You have everything to gain.

negative plus

I used to love her so much,

Back in the days, she'd drive me so nuts

One touch, lips and eyelashes

The reason why I act so anxious

My passion, you took my breath away

Made me turn around like a fade-away

And you could tell I was attracted

Just by the way I reacted

It was love at first sight

I never seen a smile so bright

I never seen eyes so heavenly

Make my heart beat to your melody…

I want to make you all mine

We can be partners in crime

We can be Bonnie and Clyde

If I can have you by my side

Fantasies, of you right next to me

What else can it be, but destiny…

Your lips are petals of roses

Your fragrance left me in hypnosis

Your body so soft and lovely

I just want to make you love me

But I could never make you trust me

And that's what makes it all so ugly.

I used to love her so much,

And take my time with her, no rush

One touch, eyelashes and lips

Hard to resist, you got me convinced

That love could exist, no need to insist,

Or explain why it is, that I'm feeling like this

I never met one so beautiful

And ever heard a voice so musical

The words I hear are music to my ears

I want to mix you down like a sound engineer

I want to master you and produce you

And copyright you so nobody else could use you

You're the number one song on my playlist

Treat you like a Classic and bump you for ages

You're precious like the words on my pages

The grooves of your body got me feeling sensations

You got me feeling so poetic,

I want to write it down so I will not forget it

Fantasies of you right next to me

What else can it be, but destiny…

Your body so soft and lovely

I just want to make you love me

But I could never make you trust me

And that's what makes it all so ugly.

That's why I got music to love me

 I think that's the only one thinking of me

Turn a negative into a plus

Because these are the things-

That happen to us.

Para Ya-Ya

TOUCH

If I could touch you

It would be with words

The curves of your mind

Caressed by my verbs

Read my lips and my tongue

As they speak spells of love

To your ears and your neck

Feel my breath down your legs

Like the tips of my nails

As you sit on the bed

With your chin tilted back

And my thoughts in your head

When your blood starts to rush

Then your love wants to bust

And you're drenched up with lust

Then you've felt my words' touch.

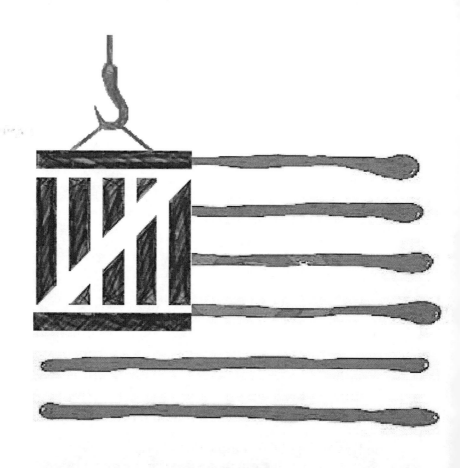

STRUGGLEGUM

Products of Adversity

If I didn't have struggle in my life, I wouldn't have the proof that I am a strong person. For without struggle, no one could ever test his or her ability to overcome. So thank your higher power on an everyday basis, for granting you the honor of being able to prove to yourself that you are a strong person. Struggle is a blessing.

US

Nothing looks sweet in the fridge…

Animal crackers and water it is

Nothing looks good in the kitchen…

Animal crackers, water and "Simpsons"

We're in it to survive, we don't need much

Animal crackers and water for US.

131

PEN

Shadow of myself tattooing on paper

Curves of my fingers hug and caress you

Pen

With me have been

Different color

Different skin, but still

My quill

Proof of my skill

Weapon of will

Kill the noise

Kill . . . there's silence to fill

Build me a temple or castle on Mexican hills

Where sunset spills shadows from trees

Plastic container of dreams

My pen

Showing the world the content within

Like clear bottles of gin

Serve me a portion, abortion of sin

Pen

In my pocket with money I spend

A jewel of a tool or a gem

In the hand of the shiniest men

From the vast to the tiniest end

Couldn't buy me the time we have spent

Or deny me the life we have skinned

The most loyal and grimiest friend

Locked in me, but not locked in the pen

My pen

Giving birth to a song

We compose love and decompose thoughts just the same

And at last,

Once your task you have fulfilled

And all the black, red, or blue venom spilled

I offer your corpse to the Goddess of Swords

Tossed towards the sky til the universe ends

But on dark and still tomorrows

We shall meet again.

5-17-2012

PX

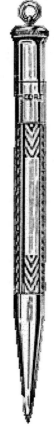

Good-lookin'

God granted me a happy day,

Without help from the county or Sallie Mae

Who said God doesn't love me

Because I don't go to church on Sunday

But smoke in my alleyway on Wednesday? ...

When God gave me a blessed day

Feeling like I know all the answers on test day

Or like I just got an A on my essay

But I still feel the need to ask this question...

For many years I've walked round' the world with an attitude,

So why do I deserve this gratitude?

When I smoke a pack of cigarettes everyday

And yet still God granted me a happy day...

Even though I have bills that I haven't paid

And I curse twenty times on an average day

Plus I have bad habits and profane thoughts

And I keep going back to the same spots,

I go to mass every other Ash Wednesday

But yet and still God gave me a blessed day.

When the devil tempted me successfully to drink excessively

I still woke up the next day,

When I'm broke, walking on a tight-rope, down to my last smoke, chin down to my chest-plate,

Just when I'm about to give in, I ask him for advice and he shows me the best way,

I saw the light shine on the worst day of my life and it turned out to be like the best day.

Stressed out, going through it in my alley-way,

But thankful, God granted me a happy day.

7.12.11

Underdog

Be an inspiration not an imitation
And take on the world with no intimidation.
Keep a long reach without limitation,
You never know the extent of your destination.
Never give in when life becomes painful,
When life becomes cruel, unpleasant and hateful.
Stabbed in the heart by those you thought faithful,
Power within keeps you balanced and stable.
Time is the cure for the wounds we endure,
The remedy making us strong and secure.
Scars are the photos of memories past,
Although they might fade, they always shall last.
No matter the baggage, keep walking the road,
Regardless how heavy the troubles you hold;
And never forget the lessons of history,
Sometimes the underdog leaves with the victory.
2/10/2010

New America

Let us play monopoly,

Instead of money let's use heads

I got 12 million

Soldier and civilian

Men, Women, and Children

In every state and every building

I am the AUTHORITY

You are the minority

I am the Wizard

You are the Dorothy

We shall exercise

Our Revolutions

So you memorize

The execution

We the enterprise

Of evolution

Thou shall terrorize our Institution-

-NO LONGER!

Witness the Weak grow str0NGER

Sir, I am relieving YOU of your Command,

With side-arm in hand

Surrender your Land

I AM,

The New American.

1-27-11

THE DEVIL IS BUSY

The devil is busy
   Working on us,
Trying so hard
   To supply us with drugs,
He works overtime
   Late nights, even weekends,
Nine to five job
   When I'm fighting my demons.
The devil is busy
   Working on us,
Working so hard
   To fulfill us with lust,
I see his workspace
   On every one's face,
The devil is busy
   He doesn't take breaks,
The devil does volunteer-
   Work in my hood,
And talks to the bad boys
   When they're doing good.
The devil is working
   With all of my friends

Giving them drugs

    In exchange for their ends

The devil has come

    To my home with a blunt,

The devil must be

    Employee of the month.

  1-6-06

Things

Sometimes I come across people
Who want to talk to me about things
I don't really feel like talking about,
So I let them know yo'…
I came to talk about real things.
They want to talk about background checks
They want to talk about court fees,
Restitution fees and fee waivers
And a copy of your most recent income tax form
They want to talk about my right to remain silent
I rather talk about my freedom of speech and how much
Will they pay me to teach
I came to talk about some real things.
They want to talk about TMZ,
They want to talk about they're sister's relationship
They want to talk about "send me your resume"
I already sent it the day before yesterday,
Let's talk about me getting paid today, strictly business;
I came to talk about real things.
They want to talk about downloads and barcodes
And all the dumb shit they can do on their "smart phones".
They want to talk about the war on drugs while Lindsay
Lohan does lines of coke in the house of blues' ladies room,
in front of the perfume lady…
They want to talk about on-line dating
I want to talk about the reasons why our schools are failing
Whose fault is it, and how fast can we fix it?
Who really runs the whole district,
And why are kids being labeled autistic

Just because they think outside the box,
Isn't that being artistic?
They want to talk about student loans and budget cuts
And layoffs?
Let's talk about payoffs, and why I put in work on Labor
Day and on my day-off.
I'm trying to teach these kids how to build things,
I came to talk about real things.
7.12.11

Truth

Read it or not, take it serious or mock it
Truth is truth
Always is, that which is
The actuality of things
Not to be altered or fabricated
The truth
That which, shall set you free
From the powers that be
A lie's worst enemy
Word to the wise, wise to the word
Never absurd, should always be heard
The truth
Relief to those who never knew it
A treasure for those who pursue it
Blessed are those who live by it
And never deny it
The truth
That which is factual
And cannot be denied
That from which
You cannot hide
The truth.

RUSH

Living in a wild
Adrenaline rush
Nicotine and caffeine
In all that I touch
Living in a rush
And never slow down
Wishing that I could
But I don't know how.
Rushing spot to spot
And place to place
Seeing myself
In every different face
Like a soldier in a War
Alone or with a fleet,
Losing track of my Victories,
Counting my defeats.
Objective is to conquer
All that I touch
Living in an endless
Adrenaline rush.

WHATTA DAY

What a day!

Nothing is beautiful today.

Can't think straight,

Can't hear the birds sing…

I came to the point

Of the things we've destroyed,

Annoyed by the sun

Seeking help from a joint.

Joy is not in me today,

No smile, no talk

Not even a reason to walk

No words to say, just pray

So that tomorrow won't be like today.

WETBACK

I'm the wetback, my water soaked shoes left a wet track
I got deported twice, but that was just a minor setback
Cause I'm strong like the current of the Colorado River
The tone of my courage made the border patrol shiver
I been through all the borders: El Paso, Tijuana,
Agua Prieta, Palomas, I move like smoke of marihuana
I'm smooth and unnoticed,
Some label me as Illegal
But if they would really notice,
I'm a reflection of their ego
I'm the reason why the Government created Border Patrol
They already took our land but they'll never take my soul
I was blind to the fact that this land belonged to me
Now I'm a slave in the place where my ancestors were royalty
They stole my history, my beliefs, even my pride
The Jews were not the only ones to suffer genocide
Now I have to sneak in to the land that I once ruled…
They told us were Illegal, now I know that we were fooled
What's my name? Where am I from?
I know that you don't know
That's why you label me simply as a U.F.O…
An alien, an Unidentified Foreign Object,
But you should think twice
About the words that you select
I'm the wetback, son of the rain and the pain
My brain remains trapped by an invisible chain
Society is my prison, from the water I have risen
I'm not being treated fair, why won't anybody listen?
Borders are just stupid reasons made by Man
To have land to their name and to have the upper hand

The government's a backstabbing, land thieving crook,
Why don't they write about that in the history book?
But the words I say are senseless,
You can never believe me
Because I'm trapped and defenseless
In the "Land of the Free"…
I'm the Wetback,
My water soaked shoes left a wet track,
I got deported twice, but that was just
A minor setback.

Outcast's Prayer

Dear Lord, thank you for another day of life

For giving me the chance to distinguish wrong from right

Thank you for the courage and the will to understand

That the challenges I face will make me a stronger man

Thank you for being there when nobody seemed to care

For giving me your bread when nobody else would share

Forgive me for the things I do, that bring you tears and pain

For promising I'll change yet my ways remain the same

Thank you for your friendship and guidance when I'm lost

Even after I deserted you when you most needed me

Sorry for abandoning you there upon that cross

Although when I was trapped, you're the one who set me free

Thank you for this gift you gave me to express myself

For blessing me with hope when I cried because I failed

Thanks for sitting next to me when I am all alone

The world had turned its back, and you took me in your home

Thank you for the comfort on those sad and painful nights

For guiding me in darkness when there wasn't any lights

Tonight while I'm asleep, take a peek inside my soul

And you'll find a thank you note,

From this weed that grew from snow,

Amen.

𝔖mile

It is a beautiful thing to be hated, for it reminds us that at least in some way, someone is thinking about us. This reminds us with certainty of our own self-worth.

On a pale, winter morning, a young Lady came to my study with inquiries regarding my craft. I told her that it is similar to that of Dr. Victor Frankenstein's through Mary Shelly. 'Tis the dark things we create which bring us closer to our creator, for he too created such beautiful monsters. Humans are like French fries, and the Lord's touch is our own Ketchup

Darkitecture (därk ′kitèk-tûr)

Dark: *destitute of light; not reflecting light; wholly black or grey; producing gloom; unenlightened, mentally or physically; obscure; untried; of a brunette complexion.*

Architecture: *the science or Art of building; the method or style of building; construction; workmanship.*

> ## The Art of Making Monsters

Words are similar to bricks, for they too are able to create monuments that demonstrate the creative power of Man's imagination. Some Men take thousands of bricks and create Universities; others take the same amount of bricks and create prisons.

Words are like bricks.

Regicide

Disconnected, misdirected,

Ethnocentric things;

Treason is the reason-

For this season, Killing Kings.

Servitude and bondage-

Fill the pillows of my dreams;

They who named us slaves,

We made widows of their Queens.

Muted bells of slavery,

Freedom never rings

Still we long to fly

With these amputated wings.

Treaty of the greedy-

Take the city from the needy;

Scorned and shackled hands

Dress your castles in graffiti.

Still while undeveloped,

Took the venom from our stings;

Since I'm seldom seen,

Tell them "I'll be Killing Kings". 3-21-12

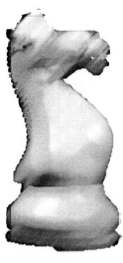

Aggravated

I am a performer of Road rage in a traffic jam of souls
Today's phrase: don't fuck with me
I'm roaming on zombie mode through an 85 degree
Fahrenheit, concrete labyrinth
I'm so moody, jazz can't soothe me
My head is a cactus-filled desert and my
Heart beats are a never ending drum solo
I am amateur Surrealism in a world of sarcastic art critics
I am tan play-do with shoe prints stuck on inner city
sidewalks
Aggravated
I am misspelld words in a letter of recommendation
I am the elegant arrogance of Mitt Romney's smirk
I am peanut shell debris on the front teeth of life's smile
I'm stuck
In the traffic jam of souls
I am the road rage of old age
Annoyed in isolation
I am a victim of last night's vengeance
I am Garofalo's poem from Chappelle's *Half-baked*
I am the love child of Henry Kissinger and Eeor from Winnie
the pooh
I am the hip-hop version of blues
I am the return of the Fannie pack
I am Charles Monroe, a.k.a. Kidd Kardashian: Inventor of
Dope nicknames
I'm crazy as fuck, but I'm not,
I am aggravated.

PISSED

In my Microsoft office.
I'm attempting neural control of my central nervous system
But I'm a Whirlwind right now.
Spinning in the waters of my deepest regrets
I
Am
Pissed
My hands' earth quakes
I'm volcanic right now. I'm Adrian's brother, Pauli right now
homey
Pissed
Tongue over matter, I am hurricane activity in my backyard
The origin of manmade madness I'm Darwin Sigmund Luther
King Chávez Hussein Jr.
In a Revolutionary Republican public
The recessive allele fucking up the evolution of my species
I'm-
Vision fragments from broken retinas
Of
Refrigerator kitchen magnets that spell my graffiti name
backwards
E-Z-E-L-P
PHANTASM at my HOOD BAPTISM
I was baptized twice
Once by my momma
Once by my drama.
Once, I even felt like baptizing my self
I did all this
And I
Was Pissed.   5-16-12

We the Gifted

We the gifted, We the cursed
Live through life so unrehearsed
We the different, We the odd
In the shadows of our God
We the gifted, We the blessed
Witnessed people at their best
We phantasms, We the cursed
Sent to dwell amongst the worst
We the gifted, We the cursed
Are enslaved in golden words
We the odd, We the different
From normality restricted
We the mad, We the sane
With a tolerance for pain
We the best and the worst
We the gifted, We the cursed.

PALE MESSENGER

A locust approaches.
Flying, venomous roaches
Pope Benedict's coaches
Searching for He' who indulges
And seeks for those evil promotions
Causing the people commotions
Hooked under mental hypnosis
Wired with different components
I tell you,
A locust approaches.
Men with the deepest emotions
Cannot become your consultants
Filled with the weakest devotion
Servants who wish they were Sultans,
Serpents still hiss in the darkness
Bitches still piss in the carpets
And Women still bitch in apartments
I tell you,
A locust approaches.
Good Friday Dining on blowfish
Smelling the scent from the Orchids
Feeling the Earth as it orbits
Drain all the venom from hornets
Make soldiers out of all Orphans
And get ready
For the Locust.

HELL'EN

Enter the home of the devil
The court on the sixteenth floor
Hell is called child support
Ink I.V. is life support
Trails of patients wait impatient
For the remedy to tame them
A sacred angel kissed my soul
And so, I woke from dreams of smoke
Into a realm of wicked beings
Where even blind Men can see things
In our dreams, we live our fears
Spider webs sparkle with tears
Liquid fire burns my belly
And I must survive through hell
And support that child as well
As I toss seeds to the pigeons
Bats from caves must also feed
With their eyes filled up with greed
They turn Sunday into dark night
Here they come I hear their wings. 3-14-02

The Beginning

I am the evil spawn

Scum, drug, rusty gun

Deceased slum

Deaf, blind, and dumb

Don't give a fuck, son-

Of a tranquilizer gun

Sick, twisted, fuckhead

Drunk, shit talkin'

Flu-carrying', eat a vegetarian

Drink the blood of an Aryan

Dissecting an alien,

Terrorizing a barbarian's family-

I am

The man without a master plan

Burning crosses outside the office-

Of the klu-klux-klan

I am,

Raw, catguts underneath the bus,

Loogies on a maggot burger,

Ketchup, mayo, puss

I'm the alley guy

Doing drive-bye's on the antichrist

With the flip of a book

And the stroke of a crook

Who never took

A second look

Just decided to write it

And eye did.

Bitches hide behind their text

And cry about their ex

Lying to the next

Supplying to their eggs

I'm denying them their rest

No rest for the wicked

That was the beginning

And this is the ending.

The Ending.

MIDNIGHT SUNRISE

Silence describes me
Jealousy follows me
Angels try searching
But can't seem to find me

Envy tries me
But cannot define me
Misery sees me
And sits down beside me

Lust is a fan of me
Craves and desires me
Greed has nothing for me
But just admires me

Vengeance is out for me
Hate has no love for me
Truth always lied to me
And trust always doubted me

Pain seems to comfort me

Loneliness is company

Happiness cries for me

Life still dies for me

Betrayal is my friend

Peace is my enemy

Depression makes me laugh

And patience wants me desperately

Silence sings songs for me
Solitude hunts for me

Poverty pays for me

Virgins make love to me

Ears can't listen
Lips can't speak
Fingers can't feel
And the eyes can't see,

When you're Senseless.

STORMS

Lost in a storm,
Trying to get home
But not knowing which way is home
And which way is wrong
Waiting for the chance to pluck the flower
And remove her from her garden
So that she may bloom inside my room
Before her petals harden;
But that's just a dream
And then I wake up
Drenched in the cold
I walk through the storm
In the dark with no route
Everything I knew is gone
Except the song that I sing to be strong…
"Things are gonna get easier",
And tears become smiles,
If only for a moment.
It's a long way home,
So I must continue walking
Through the never ending raindrops
Til I reach familiar streets.
Then I dwell in thoughts of then
When she made those smiles at me
It appeared as if the Lord
Gave me my childhood again.

Until then, I did not know
Why this life was granted to me
Til I saw the reflecting lights
Rushing from her black, diamond eyes
Now I laugh when she laughs
And I hurt when she is hurt
Every night without her
Is like tsunamis in the darkness
Quiet and destructive
And yet, without a righteous reason.
As the seasons, pass above me
Like freeway signs they go,
Nowadays I walk through storms
Hoping still, to see your face
Every day the sky is gray
And the clouds are here to stay.
I try to be strong,
But at times I feel weak
Alone with a dream
And your smile in my heart
You are worth searching for,
You are worth all the rain
You are worth having love
That cannot be explained.
My delight and my pain,
Walking, lost in the storm
Looking for you,
So we won't be alone.

DAY of the DOG

Tortilla chips and .40 Glocks

Living like a Lion-Fox

A bitch's mind is always vicious

So conniving and suspicious

She accuses you of things

That she does with all her flings

If they beat you at their game

Do them bitches just the same

Send them back from where they came

Let them practice what they claim

Let them bleed in see through panties

With their memberships to Balley's

Heartless bitches' pedigree

Show you what they hate to see

All those puppies ain't for me

A bitch is what they aim to be

They are dogs but not like us

Never seen a bitch with nuts

Maybe once but it don't count

When the nuts are in her mouth

That's the type of bitch I like

No pretendo, only pipe

Bitches, don't believe the hype!

You could never reach my height

See, you must've missed the flight

So I came to dim the light

All you bitches think you're bright

Til I bring them into darkness

Bitches always think they're right

In their universe of wrongness

But I see you wicked bitches

I can see you nice and clear

Only thing that's strictly business

Is your pussy-hole's career

Must be hard to be sincere

When a lie is so convenient

When the punishment's severe

Then the bitches are obedient

So I've learned to deal with bitches

And concluded I don't need them

Cause I know they are disloyal

And they bite the hand that feeds them

Buck'um and leave them

Or lead'um to riches

But never believe them

Ungrateful Bitches.

Windy Thursday

Beat the devil at hi*ss* craft
That apothecary math,
Beat the devils wrath with them formats like Sylvia Plath's'.
Some do wrong, while others write,
Those who seem to be that type,
Be the type that likes to type,
We beat the devil at hi*ss* craft,
Epitaph his soul in half
And laugh, and cry,
And live, and write,
And wrong, and left,
And Back to right
Til we circulate the light.
As the wind escapes my person
With a form of nonchalantness
Only falling stars possess;
And December comes to touch me
With its cold, and windy fingertips
Making ladies wanna snuggle harder in that
Starter hooded sweater, 400 strokes away
From the eleventh-thousand letter,
Tonight, I beat the devil.
12-1-11

T.I.M.E.

I'm running out of time sometimes I can feel it

Two hands turning clockwise I can see them

All I have is time so I time these sheets

Precisely on time before time completes.

Time is money, but in time it's funny

Cause' sometimes we just waste time like money

Time: a punishment for an inmate

When all you have is time, it becomes your cellmate.

Right place, at the wrong time

Time after time, happens all the time

Time crisis, there's a time for everything,

But sometimes there's hardly time for anything.

I'm running out of time, sometimes I can feel it

Trying to kill time, but just can't kill it

It is highly difficult to be time wise,

Failed attempts to pass the time, because time flies.

Maybe is a sign of the times

Hard times, one times, working part-time,

Trying to take time, but time keeps slipping

The sands in the hourglass keep dripping

Time limits, but no timing this

It's about that time, you know what time it is!

We used to think time was timeless

Or that we could rewind back time, like a Timex…

...Do you know what time it is?
Do you know what time it is?
This is taking too much time,
All I want to know is who has the time?

The hands on the clock hold Glocks',

When it's time to kill, no time to chill, time stops.

I'm running out of time, sometimes I can feel it

Time running out all day by the minute

Remember the good times; forget all the bad ones,

Laugh through the sad ones; go through the mad ones

Maybe, making a track about time,

Is the only way for me to ever keep track of time...

Overtime, my clock works awkward

Backwards, lost time traveler with an odd verse,

About time, time related,

Hang time is the time we remain elevated,

Hard times is what keeps us sedated,

Can't afford to get times [x], multiplicated.

All I have is time, so I time these sheets

Precisely on time before time completes...
...Do you know what time it is?
Do you know what time it is?
T.I.M.E. - **Time Is My Enemy,**
T.**I.M.E.** - **Time Is My**...
T.I.**M.E.** - **Time Is**...
T.I.M.**E.** - **Time**...
. ..I'm out of time.

THE LATE BLOOMER

Let it be known, this is the last page. I did not choose the title of this page, instead I asked a very special Child to do the honor of naming this final page for me; at that time, I still did not have a title for this book. However, when I asked why she chose this title for this last page, her answer made me realize something; we may bloom late, but we eventually...Ketch 'up.

Adios.

P.X
12-1-11

ABOUT THE AUTHOR

The youngest of ten siblings born to immigrant parents, Carlos was the first of the Ornelas children to be born in the United States. He attended elementary school in Mexico from Kindergarten to 5th grade and did not learn to speak the English language until he attended school in the United States in 6th grade.

Carlos Ornelas has been taking part in the poetry scene in the Los Angeles area for over 10 years and has poems published in the *Voices of Compton Literary Journal.* He is a member of the *Urban Poet Society's Compton Chapter* and is involved in the L.A. underground hip-hop scene. Carlos is also a song writer with a hip-hop album under his belt and numerous guest appearances on fellow artists' projects and is constantly working on new material.

Ornelas currently resides in Los Angeles County where he is studying to be an English Professor and is working on a book of poetry in Spanish and his second poetry book in English, as well as, a few other projects still in development. When he is not writing songs or poetry, you might find Ornelas recording music at his friend's recording studio.

Next book is in the works

Coming Soon . . .